THE WAY OF CROSS

"If any want to become my followers, let them deny themselves and take up their crosses and follow me..."

Follow Jesus through The Way of the Cross, a Mary's Call original. The Stations of the Cross or the Way of the Cross, also known as the Way of Sorrows or the Via Crucis, refers to a series of images depicting Jesus Christ on the day of his crucifixion and accompanying prayers. The stations grew out of imitations of Via Dolorosa in Jerusalem which is believed to be the actual path Jesus walked to Mount Calvary. The object of the stations is to help the Christian faithful to make a spiritual pilgrimage through contemplation of the Passion of Christ. It has become one of the most popular devotions.

MARY'S CALL
P.O. Box 162
504 W. U.S. Hwy. 24
Salisbury, MO 65281

Phone: 660-388-5308
Email: maryscall@maryscall.com

www.maryscall.com

MARY'S CALL

Mary's Call is a small, not-for-profit family organization. Our ministry is to encourage prayer, especially the Rosary and Way of the Cross.

The original undertaking of Mary's Call was the production of a 15 decade Rosary tape with meditations plus six hymns. The first order for the tape was received on May 4, 1989 (Ascension Thursday).

We create Mary's Call unique books and have available bibles, rosaries, scapulars, religious books, plaques, and many other items and religious gifts. In order for items to be sold at the lowest price, every effort is made to keep production costs to a minimum and, at the same time, maintain exceptional standards.

Mary's Call remains a very small family organization and is able to operate only through the assistance (time, talent, and donations) of friends. We hope that you will receive many blessings as a result of joining us in this ministry of prayer.

Table of Contents

My Lord and my God, ... 6

THIS MAN 7

1st Station: JESUS IS CONDEMNED TO DEATH BY PILATE.. 8

2nd Station: JESUS TAKES UP HIS CROSS TO CARRY IT TO CALVARY 10

3rd Station: JESUS FALLS THE FIRST TIME......... 12

4th Station: JESUS MEETS HIS MOTHER MARY . 14

5th Station: SIMON OF CYRENE HELPS JESUS CARRY HIS CROSS 16

6th Station: VERONICA WIPES THE FACE OF JESUS WITH HER VEIL... 18

7th Station: JESUS FALLS THE SECOND TIME.... 20

8th Station: THE WOMEN OF JERUSALEM WEEP FOR CHRIST 22

9th Station: JESUS FALLS THE THIRD TIME........ 24

10th Station: JESUS IS STRIPPED OF HIS CLOTHES 26

11th Station: JESUS IS NAILED TO THE CROSS .. 28

12th Station: JESUS DIES ON THE CROSS 30

13th Station: JESUS IS TAKEN DOWN FROM THE CROSS... 32

14th Station: JESUS IS PLACED IN THE TOMB.... 34

15th Station: JESUS RISES FROM THE DEAD 36

CLOSING PRAYER 37

PROMISES MADE BY OUR LORD TO THOSE WHO HAVE DEVOTION TO THE WAY OF THE CROSS 40

TO JESUS FORSAKEN 42

TO JESUS, CROSS CARRIER 43

COME HOLY SPIRIT 44

ACT OF PERFECT CONTRITION 45

A PRAYER FOR THE FORGOTTEN DEAD 45

HOLY TRINITY PRAYER 46

ACT OF RESIGNATION 47

A PRAYER TO REDEEM LOST TIME 47

INDIFFERENCE 48

PRAYER OF ST. GERTRUDE THE GREAT 49

PRAYER FOR THE SEVEN GIFTS OF THE HOLY SPIRIT 50

PRAYER TO DEFEAT THE WORK OF SATAN 51

PRAYER TO PROTECT LIFE 53

My Lord and my God,
> under the loving eyes of our Mother,
> we are making ready to accompany you along
> this path of sorrow,
> which was the price for our redemption.

We wish to suffer all that You suffered,
> to offer you our poor, contrite hearts,
> because you are innocent, and yet
> you are going to die for us,
> who are the only really guilty ones.

My Mother, Virgin of sorrows,
> help me to relive those bitter hours
> which your Son wished to spend on earth,
> so that we, who were made from a handful
> of clay, may finally live in libertatem gloriae
> filiorum Dei, in the freedom and glory of
> the children of God.

THIS MAN

There was a Man. One sent from God,
Who came to Earth one day
To make amends for Adam's sin,
And show Mankind the way.

This Man, although from Heaven sent,
Is not but God alone;
Of virgin pure he was begot
A Man, in flesh and bone.

He is both Human and Divine.
In God He is the Son
But in majesty they're equal, for
The Father and He are one.

He came to Earth in Human form
To open Heaven's door,
And suffered all, that we might live
In Love forevermore.

His back was torn by stinging whips;
A crown of thorns He wore;
His shoulders sagged beneath the weight
Of the heavy cross He bore.

And yet through all this agony
That ended in His death;
He uttered only words of love
Unto His dying breath.

-- Vincent J. Flynn

1st Station: JESUS IS CONDEMNED TO DEATH BY PILATE

We adore you, O Christ, and we praise you Because by Your holy cross You have redeemed the world.

How often **I judge people unjustly.** Jesus forgive me for it. I see people only from the outside. You know them from the inside. Help me to leave all judgments to You. I will give them the benefit of the doubt.

As we meditate on Jesus being condemned to death, we pray for those condemned to death today, particularly, unborn children, those who receive the death penalty, and those we condemn by gossip or criticism.

**LORD, JESUS CRUCIFIED,
HAVE MERCY ON ME.**

The Way of Cross   Mary's Call

2nd Station: JESUS TAKES UP HIS CROSS TO CARRY IT TO CALVARY

We adore you, O Christ, and we praise You Because by Your holy cross You have redeemed the world.

You showed a ready **obedience** in taking up Your cross. I often forget that it takes strength to obey, not weakness. Forgive my disobedience. Since all lawful authority comes from God, I am really obeying You out of love.

As we ponder Jesus carrying His cross, we pray for the grace to carry our own crosses whether they be small or large. We pray for all people as we bear the cross of participating in unjust societies that inflict sufferings on so many peoples.

**LORD JESUS CRUCIFIED,
HAVE MERCY ON ME.**

The Way of Cross	Mary's Call

3rd Station: JESUS FALLS THE FIRST TIME

We adore you, O Christ, and we praise You Because by Your holy cross You have redeemed the world.

You fell, O Jesus, because Your human body was weak. I too am **weak** so sometimes I fall. But I will always rise and keep trying to please You, because I love You.

In Jesus' fall, we experience how truly human He became for us. As we contemplate Jesus, we pray for the grace to accept our own human weakness and the human weakness of our church. We pray that as Jesus redeemed the world by consciously accepting His human weakness and death, we may, be consciously choosing God's way for us, continue the redemption of the world.

**LORD JESUS CRUCIFIED,
HAVE MERCY ON ME.**

The Way of Cross   Mary's Call

4th Station: JESUS MEETS HIS MOTHER MARY

We adore you, O Christ, and we praise You Because by Your holy cross You have redeemed the world.

Mary's mission was to **give Christ to the world.** My mission as a Christian is to give Christ to the world. By my Christlike life I show Christ to my fellowmen. Help me to do this, O Jesus.

At this station we pray, in union with Mary, for all mothers who must watch their children suffer or die. We pray for the grace for ourselves and for all people to be able to "be with" others in their suffering and we pray for the grace to allow others to support us in our own suffering.

**LORD JESUS CRUCIFIED,
HAVE MERCY ON ME.**

The Way of Cross · Mary's Call

5th Station: SIMON OF CYRENE HELPS JESUS CARRY HIS CROSS

We adore you, O Christ, and we praise You Because by Your holy cross You have redeemed the world.

I'm too selfish, Jesus. I love myself too much. I don't love You enough. Particularly I don't **love my neighbor** enough, especially if I don't like him. A cross is lighter when two carry it. Give me a great love for my neighbor so that I will help him carry his crosses, by my kindness, in word and action.

As we observe Simon helping Jesus, we ask how ready we are to assist publicly the outcasts of our society. We pray that God's Spirit will teach us to identify with the poor, the lonely, and those not accepted in our circle of friends, our city, our country. Since Jesus and our church call us to prefer those who are poor in any way, we pray that we will make our church community a dwelling place where people, particularly the poor and marginalized, will be welcomed and feel at home.

**LORD JESUS CRUCIFIED,
HAVE MERCY ON ME.**

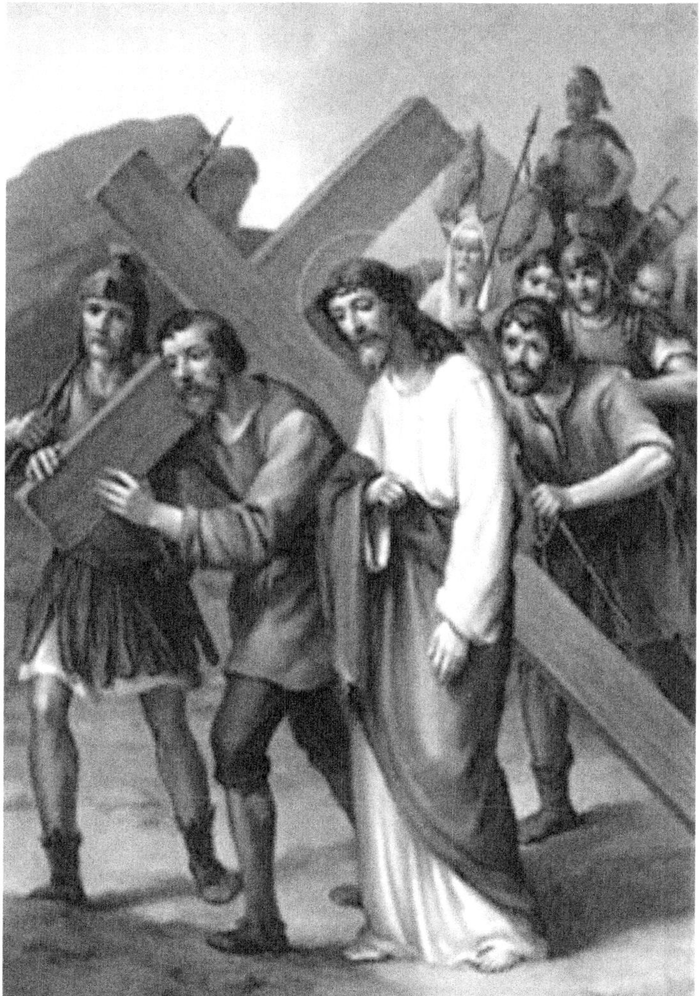

6th Station: **VERONICA WIPES THE FACE OF JESUS WITH HER VEIL**

We adore you, O Christ, and we praise You Because by Your holy cross You have redeemed the world.

Veronica had **courage,** Lord. She went fearlessly to Christ, in spite of the soldiers. I am a coward. I'm afraid to do what I should because I fear what people will think or say, ridicule, or criticize. Help me use the courage that the Holy Spirit gave my soul at Confirmation.

As we watch Veronica offer a special kindness to Jesus, we pray for the grace for ourselves, for our entire church, and for all people to respond to our neighbor - whoever the neighbor may be - with kindness and compassion, instead of with indifference.

**LORD JESUS CRUCIFIED,
HAVE MERCY ON ME.**

The Way of Cross　　　　　　　　　　Mary's Call

19

7th Station: JESUS FALLS THE SECOND TIME

We adore you, O Christ, and we praise You Because by Your holy cross You have redeemed the world.

I often fall Jesus, because **I take chances.** I expose myself to dangerous occasions of sin. Because sin is unlove I will not take chances of sinning, because I do want to love You.

As we follow Jesus, we become weary, we fall, we count the cost. We wonder if following Jesus is worth the effort; at times, we even wonder WHY we should attempt to keep trying. At this station, we pray for all of us, the grace to rise again after each fall and to live for God and for God's reign.

**LORD JESUS CRUCIFIED,
HAVE MERCY ON ME.**

The Way of Cross   Mary's Call

8th Station: THE WOMEN OF JERUSALEM WEEP FOR CHRIST

We adore you, O Christ, and we praise You Because by Your holy cross You have redeemed the world.

How many times, Jesus, have I told You that I'm **sorry** for my sins? But how many times have I been sorry enough to change my ways? If I really love someone, I try my best not to hurt them. And if I hurt them, I am deeply sorry, and firmly determined not to hurt them again. Is that the way I act to You, my God?

As we contemplate Jesus consoling the women who came to offer Him compassion, we learn again how Jesus takes time, even in the midst of the most important work of His earthly life, to be concerned about others. We ask for the grace for ourselves and for all people, to dare to take time for others, even in the midst of our busyness and important activities.

**LORD JESUS CRUCIFIED,
HAVE MERCY ON ME.**

The Way of Cross   Mary's Call

9th Station: JESUS FALLS THE THIRD TIME

We adore you, O Christ, and we praise You Because by Your holy cross You have redeemed the world.

I get **discouraged,** Lord, when I fall again and again. But never let me lose hope. Never let me despair. Your strength and Your love for me can do what I cannot do alone, I will get this divine strength and love regularly through prayer and the sacraments. You said: "My grace is enough for you." I trust You, Lord.

Each of us, in our own way, falls over and over again. Our experience tells us that when we most feel our weakness and need, we depend more on God. We pray for ourselves and for our entire church that we might really believe God's word, that God's power is at its best in us when we are weak and seemingly helpless; we pray, too, that we might, both in times of strength and in times of weakness, trust totally in God's grace and power.

**LORD JESUS CRUCIFIED,
HAVE MERCY ON ME.**

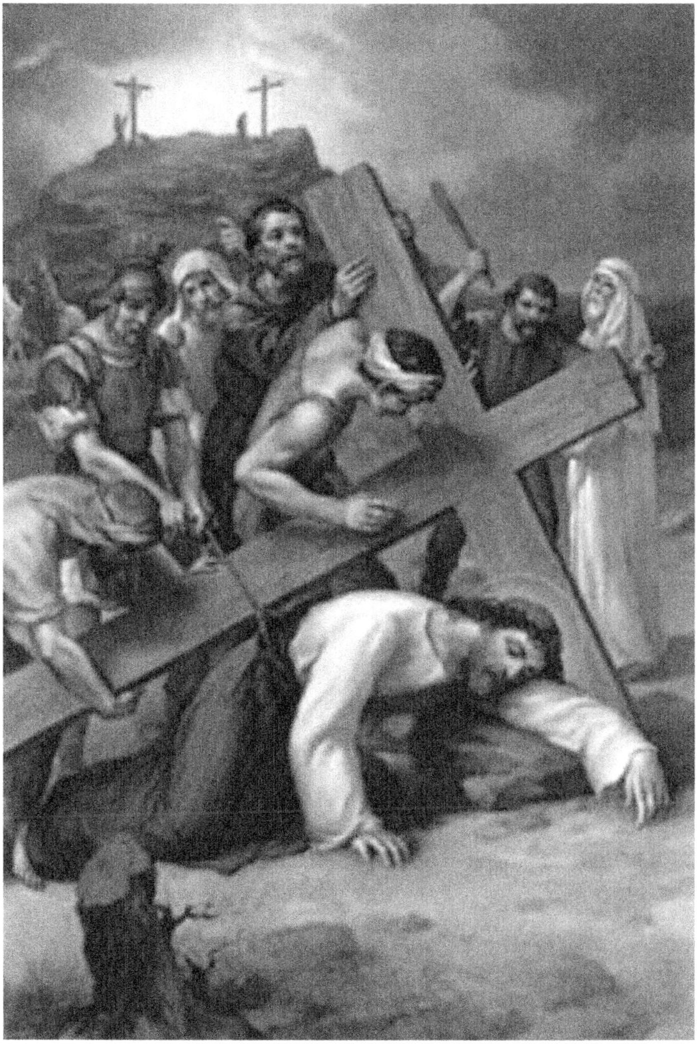

10th Station: JESUS IS STRIPPED OF HIS CLOTHES

We adore you, O Christ, and we praise You Because by Your holy cross You have redeemed the world.

How much do I value **modesty and purity,** Lord, My body was made by God, and it is good. He gave me the power of giving life and giving love, two most precious gifts. My body is sacred. I will reverence it. I will reverence the bodies of others. Especially, since You come into my body in Holy Communion, and **God is in me!**

As we ponder Jesus being stripped of His garments, we pray for those who are stripped of their jobs, their possessions, their human dignity and their selfworth. We pray particularly for those whom we have "stripped" in any way by our thoughts, words, or actions. We ask our God, too, that we and the entire church might be stripped of anything that keeps us from union with God.

**LORD JESUS CRUCIFIED,
HAVE MERCY ON ME.**

The Way of Cross　　　　　　　　　　Mary's Call

11th Station: JESUS IS NAILED TO THE CROSS

We adore you, O Christ, and we praise You Because by Your holy cross You have redeemed the world.

If I have nails driven through the palms of my hands and through my feet, I would probably faint from the suffering. I hate **suffering.** But so did you, Lord. I know, however, that I must suffer sometimes in my life. I can either waste it by resenting it, or I can accept it, out of love for You and to make up for my sins. Then it has a saving value, as Your suffering did.

Let us watch, listen and experience Jesus being nailed to the cross. Spontaneously, we ask: "Am I, are we, worth all of this? Can we be so loved?" Jesus responds consistently: "You are my chosen one in whom my soul delights … I give Egypt for your ransom … because you are precious in my eyes, because you are honored and I love you, I give all in exchange for you, all peoples in return for your life … I am with you." (Isaiah 42, 43, passim) We pray to truly believe this good news!

**LORD JESUS CRUCIFIED,
HAVE MERCY ON ME.**

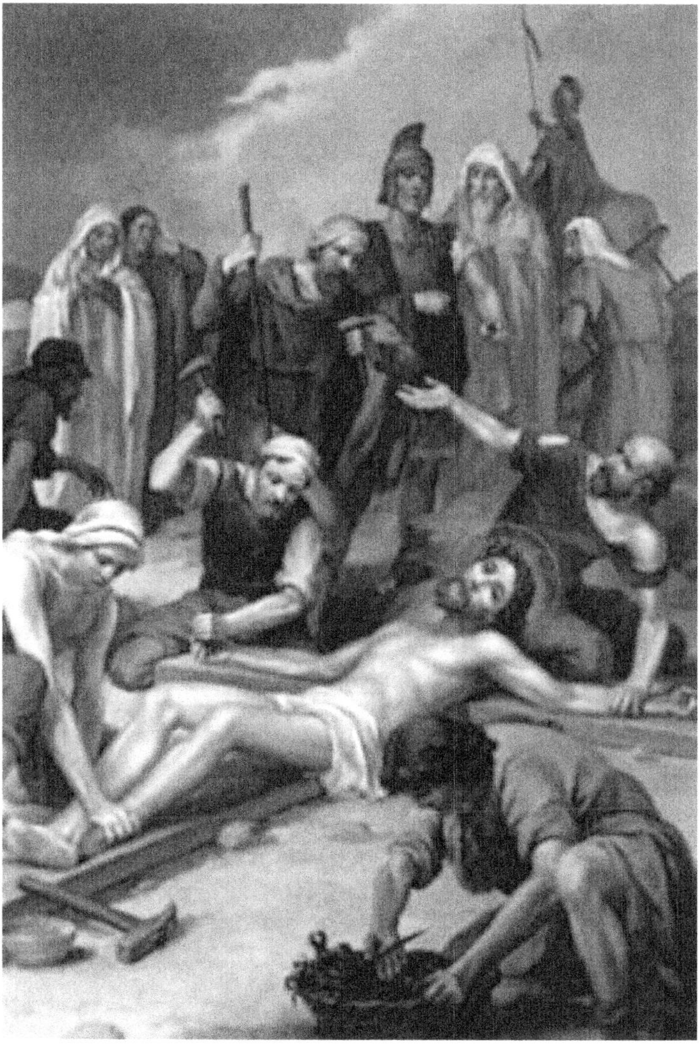

12th Station: JESUS DIES ON THE CROSS

We adore you, O Christ, and we praise You Because by Your holy cross You have redeemed the world.

You died, O Jesus, **I will die** too. I don't know when. I don't know where. I don't know how. My earthly life will end. My eternity will begin. You said we should always be ready. I will stay in Your love and grace always. Then I will always be ready.

How easy it is to carry hurts in our hearts, to fail to forgive, particularly those involved in the situations that cause us most pain. We pray for the grace to truly forgive, especially the grace to forgive ourselves. We pray, too, for those who are dying at this moment, especially those who suffer a violent death and those who are dying of aids and of cancer.

**LORD JESUS CRUCIFIED,
HAVE MERCY ON ME.**

The Way of Cross					Mary's Call

13th Station: JESUS IS TAKEN DOWN FROM THE CROSS

We adore you, O Christ, and we praise You Because by Your holy cross You have redeemed the world.

Your **sacred body** is laid in the arms of Your Mother. She receives You with love and reverence. I receive Your sacred Body in the Eucharist. Help me always to receive You with love and reverence, for You are my God!

Mary probably held the dead body of Jesus in her arms when it was taken from the cross. Even in her grief and anguish, she probably offered to her God, the son she loved so dearly. Since God wants us, that is, all that we have and are, we offer all and pray for ourselves and for all people the grace to "let go" of all we hold most dear if God asks this of us.

**LORD JESUS CRUCIFIED,
HAVE MERCY ON ME.**

The Way of Cross　　　　　　　　　　Mary's Call

14th Station: JESUS IS PLACED IN THE TOMB

We adore you, O Christ, and we praise You Because by Your holy cross You have redeemed the world.

Your **work is done.** Your Resurrection to new life will climax it. You have redeemed the world. You have offered the greatest gift: Yourself. You have shown the greatest love. Your life brought good to all people, even into eternity. Help me to live a life of love. Love for you, my God. Love for my fellowman, too. Help me to give my **greatest gift, myself,** to you and to them, in love. Then my work will be done. I too will have brought much good to people, even into eternity.

Like Joseph, we, today, reverence the bodies of the dead. As we contemplate the dead body of Jesus being laid in the tomb, we realize that Jesus died so that His spirit might be in each of us. We pray for ourselves and for all Christians, that we might reverence one another, because the living presence of Jesus is within each of us.

**LORD JESUS CRUCIFIED,
HAVE MERCY ON ME.**

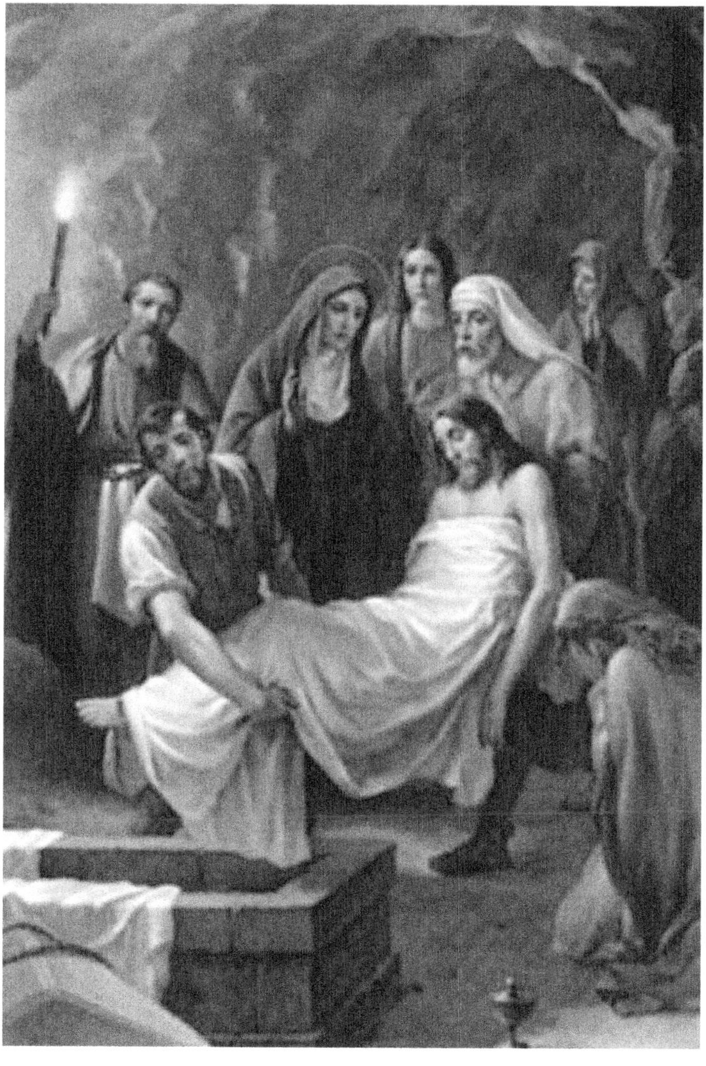

15th Station: JESUS RISES FROM THE DEAD

We adore you, O Christ, and we praise You Because by Your holy cross You have redeemed the world.

We cannot contemplate the suffering and death of Jesus without also contemplating His Resurrection. Suffering, death and new life are one mystery, even though, in our humanity, we would like to experience new life without going through suffering and death.

The crown must be earned through the cross. Jesus' victory of the Resurrection followed three days of sadness and depression. Jesus conquered darkness - He overcame death. Through His victorious Resurrection we can overcome our own failures and trials. Jesus is always at our side giving us courage and strength to rise to new life with Him.

**LORD JESUS CRUCIFIED,
HAVE MERCY ON ME.**

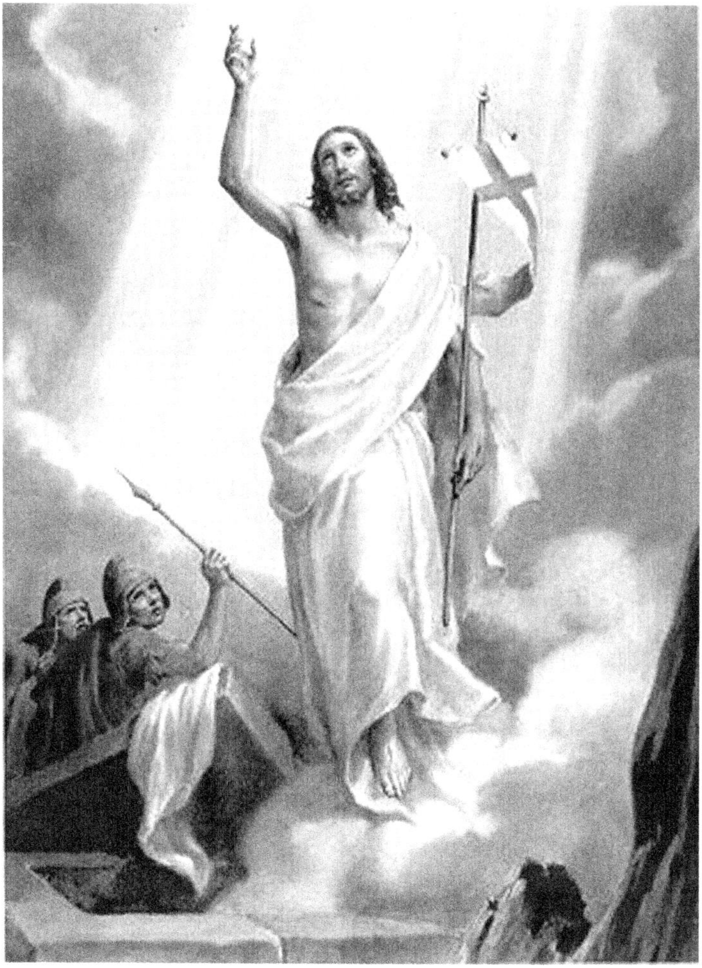

CLOSING PRAYER

*"Dying – You destroyed our death,
Rising – You restored our life …"*

O God, these simple but awe inspiring words used at the Consecration of the Mass reveal the meaning of our own life here on earth. You have planned for our salvation. While following Jesus' path of suffering, we have prayed for Your graces to enable us to have faith in our own resurrection from our human life of crosses and trials. We believe that our departed family and friends are united with You. We pray now that You will keep us always faithful to You so that we too may one day be united with You and them forever. Amen

Is the Way of the Cross the way of every person's life? Doesn't every life have suffering, falls, hurts, rejections, condemnations, death, burial ... and resurrection?

It has been a Catholic tradition through the centuries to meditate on the Way of the Cross, so that it becomes our way of life.

The Way of the Cross is not a sad devotion. Christian joy has its roots in the shape of a cross. If the Passion of Christ is a way of pain, it is also a path of hope leading to certain victory. You should realize that God wants you to be glad and that, if you do all you can, you will be happy, very, very happy, although you will never for a moment be without the Cross. But that Cross is no longer a gallows. It is the throne from which Christ reigns. And at His side, His Mother, our Mother too. The Blessed Virgin will obtain for you the strength that you need to walk decisively in the footsteps of her Son.

PROMISES MADE BY OUR LORD TO THOSE WHO HAVE DEVOTION TO THE WAY OF THE CROSS

1. I'll grant everything that's asked of Me with Faith, when making the Way of the Cross.

2. I promise Eternal Life to those who pray from time to time, The Way of the Cross.

3. I'll follow them everywhere in life and I'll help them, especially at the hour of death.

4. Even if they have more sins than blades of grass in the fields, and grains of sand in the sea, all of them will be erased by The Way of the Cross. (Note: This promise does not eliminate the obligation to confess all mortal sins, and this, before we can receive Holy Communion.)

5. Those who pray The Way of the Cross often, will have a special glory in Heaven.

6. I'll deliver them from Purgatory, indeed if they go there at all, the first Tuesday or Friday, after their death.

7. I'll bless them at each Way of the Cross, and My blessing will follow them everywhere on earth and, after their death, in Heaven for all Eternity.

8. At the hour of death I won't permit the devil to tempt them; I'll lift all power from Him in order that they'll repose tranquilly in My Arms

9. If they pray with true love, I'll make each one of them a living Ciborium in which it will please Me to pour My grace.

10. I'll fix My Eyes on those who pray The Way of the Cross often; My hands will always be open to protect them.

11. As I am nailed to the Cross, so also will I always be with those who honor Me in making The Way of the Cross frequently.

12. They'll never be able to separate themselves from Me, for I'll give them the grace never again to commit a Mortal sin.

13. At the hour of death, I'll console them with My Presence and we'll go together to Heaven. Death will be sweet to all those who have honored Me during their lives by praying The Way of the Cross.

14. My Soul will be a protective shield for them, and will always help them, whenever they have recourse.

"Jesus Mary, I Love You, Save Souls"

TO JESUS FORSAKEN

Sweet Jesus! For how many ages hast Thou hung upon Thy Cross and still men pass Thee by and regard Thee not!

How often have I passed Thee, by heedless of Thy great sorrow, Thy many wounds, Thy infinite love!

How often have I stood before Thee, not to comfort and console Thee, but to add to Thy sorrows, to deepen Thy wounds, to spurn Thy love!

Thou has stretched forth Thy hands to raise me up and I have taken those hands and bent them back on the cross.

Thou hast loved me with an infinite love, and I have taken advantage of that love to sin the more against Thee.

My ingratitude has pierced Thy Sacred Heart, and Thy heart responds only with an out-pouring of Thy love in Thy Precious Blood.

Lamb of God Who takes away the sins of the world, have mercy on me.

TO JESUS, CROSS CARRIER

O Jesus, by that Wound which Thou didst suffer on Thy shoulder from carrying Thy cross, have mercy, I entreat Thee, on those who have secret sorrows which only Thou canst know. May the memory of Thy painful Cross-bearings give them strength to carry theirs, with courage and loyalty to the end. May the thought of that secret Suffering, Thou didst endure, teach them to sanctify their hidden sorrows that they may be fruitful for Thy Glory. Amen.

COME HOLY SPIRIT

Renew My Faith
Make My Witness
For You Bolder,
My Love Deeper,
And My Prayers
Always From
My Heart.

Faith is the avenue to sanctification. Not intellectual understanding. Not money. Not your works. Just simple **faith**. How much **faith**? The **faith** of a mustard seed, so small you can hardly see it. But if you will put that little faith in the person of The Holy Spirit, your life will be changed. He will come with supernatural power into your heart. It can happen to you.

ACT OF PERFECT CONTRITION

O my God, I am heartily sorry and beg pardon for all my sins, not so much because these sins bring suffering of hell to me; but because they have crucified my loving Savior Jesus Christ and offended Your infinite goodness, I firmly resolve, with the help of Your grace to confess my sins, to do penance and to amend my life. Amen.

A PRAYER FOR THE FORGOTTEN DEAD

O merciful God, take pity on those souls who have no particular friends and intercessors to recommend them to You, who either through negligence of those who are alive or through length of time, are forgotten by all. Spare them, O Lord, and remember Your own when others forget to appeal to Your mercy. Let not the souls You have created be parted from You, their Creator.

HOLY TRINITY PRAYER

Jesus sent His Apostles forth in the name of the Blessed Trinity.

The Mother of God asks: My children, I ask you to say this prayer to the Holy Trinity every day.

Jesus says: This is a very strong and powerful prayer. Let everyone know it. Spread it around and other people will spread it. The fire of God cannot be put out. God blesses you in the name of the Father, Son and Holy Spirit. Amen.

Dear Holy Trinity, united in perfect love, You are three conceived in one Being. Oh, Holy Trinity, come down upon me for I Your poor miserable servant call upon You. Oh, Father, You are mighty and have done great things for me. I am Your servant. Use me as You wish. O, loving, caring Jesus, You have saved me from total damnation. How shall I repay Thee? Love, Peace and Joy. Dearest Holy Spirit, without You I would be lost. You give me the strength I need. Holy Trinity, I submit myself to You. Amen.

ACT OF RESIGNATION

Lord, I know not what to ask; I merely present my- self to Thee. Thou seest my miseries. Thou lovest me. Supply my needs according to Thy Mercy. I adore, without seeking to understand, Thy Holy Will. I resign myself to Thee, entirely and absolutely. I have no other desire but to do what Thou dost wish me to do. Teach me to pray, O Jesus! Pray within me Thyself. Amen.

A PRAYER TO REDEEM LOST TIME

by St. Teresa of Avila

O my God! Source of all mercy ! I acknowledge Your sovereign power. While recalling the wasted years that are past, I believe that You,
Lord, can in an instant turn this loss to gain. Miserable as I am, yet I firmly believe that You can do all things. Please restore to me the time lost, giving me Your grace, both now and in the future, that I may appear before You in "wedding garments." Amen

INDIFFERENCE

When Jesus came to Golgotha
    they hanged Him on a tree,
They drove great nails through
    hands and feet and made a Calvary.
They crowned Him with a crown of thorns;
    red were His wounds and deep,
For those were crude and cruel days,
    and human flesh was cheap.
When Jesus came to live with us
    we simply passed Him by.
We never hurt a hair of Him,
    we only let Him die;
For we had grown more tender,
    and we would not give Him pain,
We only just passed down the street,
    and left Him in the rain.
Still Jesus cried: "Forgive them
    for they know not what they do."
And still it rained the winter rain
    that drenched Him through and through.
The crowds went home and
    left the streets without a soul to see,
And Jesus crouched against a wall
    and Cried For Calvary!

PRAYER OF ST. GERTRUDE THE GREAT

Dictated by Our Lord to Release 1,000 Souls from Purgatory Each Time It Is Said

"Eternal Father, I offer Thee the Most Precious Blood of Thy Divine Son, Jesus, in union with the Masses said throughout the world today, for all the holy Souls in Purgatory. Amen."

JESUS, JESUS, JESUS

Pray for the poor souls – Your prayer will be their key to Heaven.

Our blessed Mother said at Medjugorje that when we pray for a Holy Soul by name that soul can see us.

PRAYER FOR THE SEVEN GIFTS OF THE HOLY SPIRIT

O Lord Jesus Christ, Who, before ascending into heaven, did promise to send the Holy Spirit to finish Your work in the souls of Your Apostles and Disciples – deign to grant the same Holy Spirit to me, to perfect in my soul the work of Your grace and Your love.

Grant me the Spirit of Wisdom – that I may not be attached to the perishable things of this world, but aspire only after the things that are eternal.

The Spirit of Understanding – to enlighten my mind with the light of Your divine truth.

The Spirit of Counsel – that I may ever choose the surest way of pleasing God and gaining heaven.

The Spirit of Fortitude – that I may bear my cross with You, and that I may overcome with courage all the obstacles that oppose my salvation.

The Spirit of' Knowledge – that I may know God and know myself, and grow perfect in the science of the Saints.

The Spirit of Piety – that I may find the service of God sweet and amiable.

The Spirit of Fear – that I may be filled with a loving reverence towards God and may avoid anything that may displease Him.

Mark me, dear Lord, with the sign of Your true disciples, and animate me in all things with Your spirit. Amen.

PRAYER TO DEFEAT THE WORK OF SATAN

O Divine Eternal Father, in union with your Divine Son and the Holy Spirit, and through the Immaculate Heart of Mary, I beg You to destroy the Power of your greatest enemy – the evil spirits.

Cast them into the deepest recesses of hell and chain them there forever! Take possession of your Kingdom which You have created and which is rightfully yours

Heavenly Father, give us the reign of the Sacred Heart of Jesus and the Immaculate Heart of Mary.

I repeat this prayer out of pure love for You with every beat of my heart and with every breath I take.

Amen.

I am calling you to **sincere prayer** with the heart so that every prayer of yours may be an encounter with God. In your work and in your everyday life, do put God in the first place.

Only by **prayer** can you understand and accept my messages and practice them in your life. Read Sacred Scripture, Live it, and pray to understand the signs of the time. This is a special time. I am with you to draw you close to the Heart of my Son, Jesus. I want you to be children of the light and not of the darkness. Live what I am telling you. Thank you for having responded to my call.

PRAYER TO PROTECT LIFE

Loving God, I thank you for the gift of life you gave and continue to give to me and to all of us.

Merciful God, I ask your pardon and forgiveness for my own failure and the failure of all people to respect and foster all forms of life in our universe.

Gracious God, I pray that with your grace, I and all people will reverence, protect, and promote all life and that we will be especially sensitive to the life of the unborn, the abused, neglected, disabled, and the elderly. I pray, too, that all who make decisions about life in any form will do so with wisdom, love, and courage.

Living God, I praise and glorify you
    as Father, Source of all life,
    as Son, Saviour of our lives, and
    as Spirit, Sanctifier of our lives.
Amen.

-- Sister Mary Margaret Johanning , S.S.N.D.
-- Nihil Obstat: Joseph F. Martino
-- Imprimatur: Anthony Cardinal Bevilacqua
-- Archbishop of Phila, June 1994

The Way of Cross   Mary's Call

Printed in Great Britain
by Amazon